the Bubble Wrap Queen

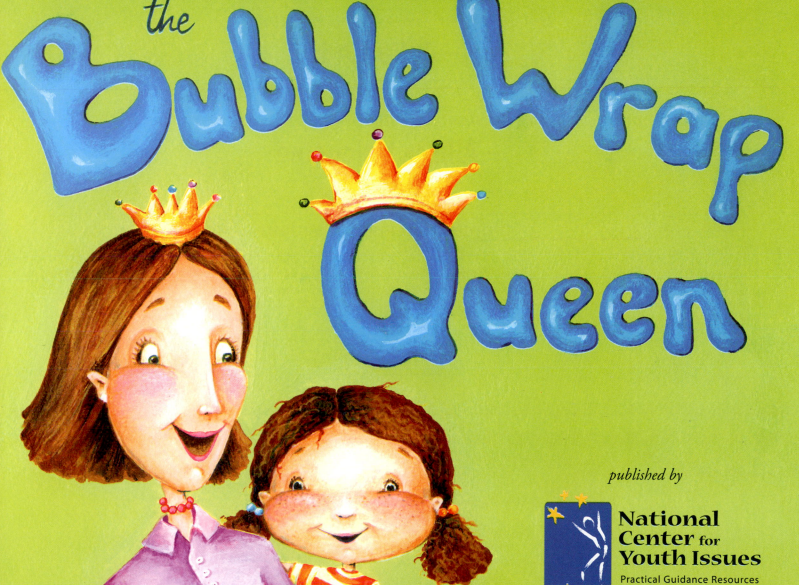

published by

National Center for Youth Issues

ncyi.org

Practical Guidance Resources
Educators Can Trust

www.ncyi.org

To Carter, for believing in me always.
– Julia Cook

To my Mom, who would have bubble-wrapped the world for me.
– Allison Valentine

Duplication and Copyright

No part of this publication may be reproduced, stored in a retrieval system or transmitted in any form by any means, electronic, mechanical, photocopy, recording or otherwise without prior written permission from the publisher except for all worksheets and activities which may be reproduced for a specific group or class. Reproduction for an entire school or school district is prohibited.

National Center for Youth Issues
Practical Guidance Resources
Educators Can Trust
ncyi.org

P.O. Box 22185
Chattanooga, TN 37422-2185
423.899.5714 • 800.477.8277
fax: 423.899.4547
www.ncyi.org

ISBN: 978-1-931636-83-4
© 2008 National Center for Youth Issues, Chattanooga, TN
All rights reserved.

Written by: Julia Cook
Illustrations and Cover Design by Contract: Allison Valentine
Page Layout by: Phillip W. Rodgers
Published by National Center for Youth Issues
Softcover

Printed by RR Donnelley, Inc.
Reynosa, Mexico
March, 2011

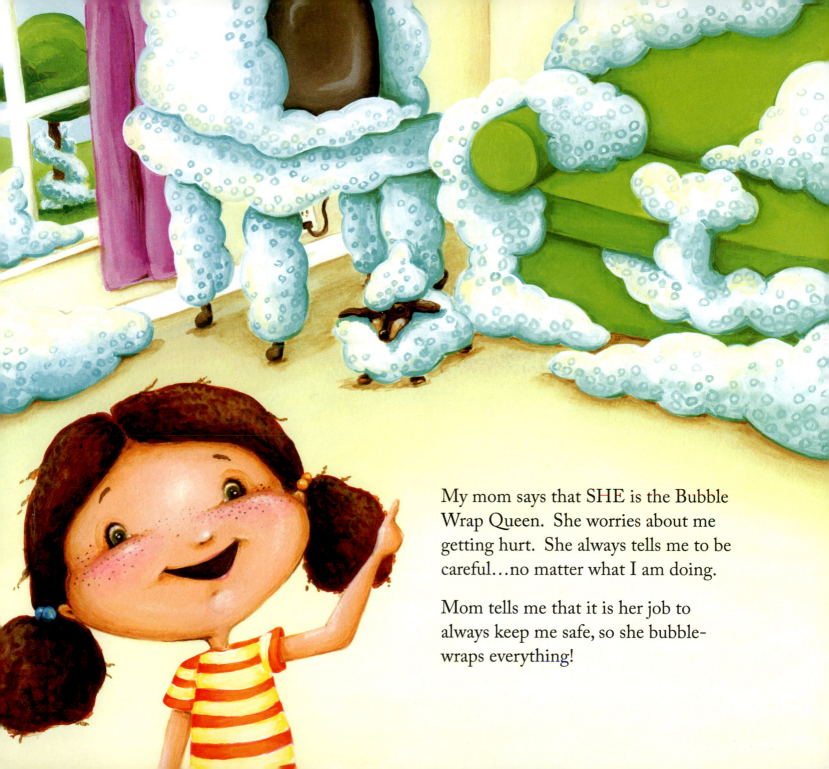

My mom says that SHE is the Bubble Wrap Queen. She worries about me getting hurt. She always tells me to be careful…no matter what I am doing.

Mom tells me that it is her job to always keep me safe, so she bubble-wraps everything!

My mom always tells me to pick my toys up off of the floor as soon as I'm finished playing with them. She doesn't want me to forget that they are there. She worries that I might trip over them and skin my knees.

The other day, my mom bubble-wrapped all of my toys, just to keep me safe.

My mom never wants me to get hurt when I play on the tricky bars at recess, so last week she went to my school and bubble-wrapped the whole playground... just to keep me safe.

If the recess teacher hadn't moved out of the way, she would have bubble-wrapped her to the slide!

Every time I get in the car to go for a ride, my mom straps me into my "auto throne" in the back seat, and then she bubble-wraps the inside of our car... just to keep me safe.

When our car ride is over, we get out of the car and my mom bubble-wraps the outside of our car so that I can't open up the doors and play inside…

"It is **never** safe to play inside of a parked car, said my mom, and I must keep you safe!"

My mom bubble-wraps everything in our house that is poisonous and harmful. She wraps up cleaners, medicines, and even our matches. It takes up a lot of her time, but she says that she will do just about anything to keep me safe.

I just love to jump on my pogo stick, but every time I do it, my mom makes me wait while she bubble-wraps everything in my play room. She even bubble-wraps the ceiling…just to keep me safe!

Whenever I go outside to ride my bike, my mom makes me put on my bike helmet and then I have to wait while she bubble-wraps our yard. She covers everything: curbs, houses, mailboxes.

One day, she even bubble-wrapped our neighbor, Mr. Wiggins... just to keep me safe.

Yesterday, my mom put bubble wrap down at the bottom of our stairs.

"What are you doing that for?" I asked. "Stairs can be dangerous!" said my mom. "You need to be careful when you go up and down the stairs. If you ever happen to trip or fall, you'll have some nice soft bubble wrap to land on."

My mom thinks of everything! She says she would bubble-wrap the whole world…just to keep me safe.

Today, my mom ran out of bubble wrap so we went to the store to buy more. They were all sold out. "I'm sorry," said the clerk. "We sold all of our bubble wrap to you."

"Oh," said my mom….

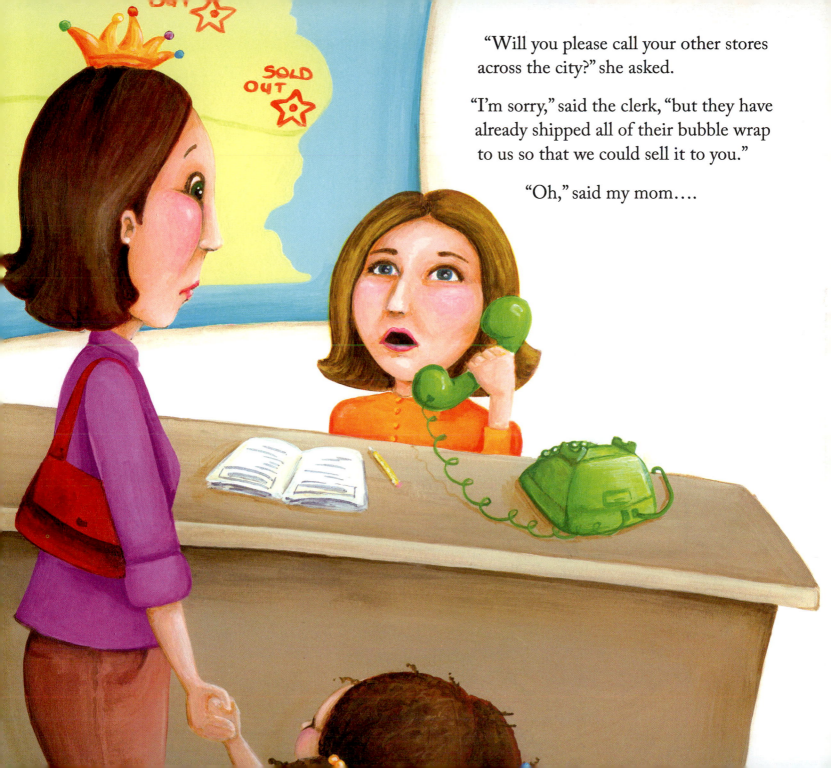

"Will you please call your other stores across the city?" she asked.

"I'm sorry," said the clerk, "but they have already shipped all of their bubble wrap to us so that we could sell it to you."

"Oh," said my mom….

"Will you please call your other stores across the state?"
she asked.

"I'm sorry," said the clerk, "but they have already
shipped all of their bubble wrap to us so that we
could sell it to you."

"Oh," said my mom....

"Will you please call your other stores across the nation?" she asked.

"I'm sorry," said the clerk, "but they have already shipped all of their bubble wrap to us so that we could sell it to you."

"Oh," said my mom….

I couldn't believe my ears! My mom had used up all of the bubble wrap in the whole country...just to keep me safe.

"Now what will you do?" I asked.

BASICS

"Well," she said, "without bubble wrap,
we'll have to go back to the…

B-A-S-I-C-S."

"The BASICS," I said. "What are they?"

"Well, **BASICS** stands for…

Be Aware and Safe
In Common Situations"

said my mom.

"Without bubble wrap, you must always remember to pick up your toys when you are finished playing with them so that you don't forget they are there and trip over them later."

"Without bubble wrap, you must be extra careful when you play on the tricky bars at school, follow the recess teacher's safety rules, and always look before you leap."

"Without bubble wrap, I will have to be a super careful driver when I strap you into your "auto throne" and take you places in the car.

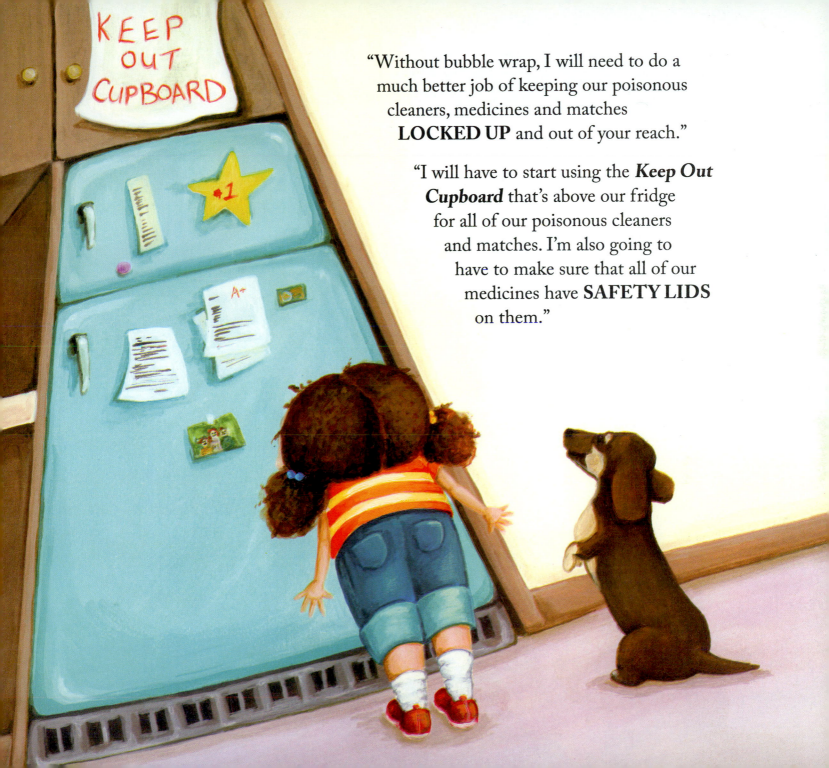

"Without bubble wrap, I will need to do a much better job of keeping our poisonous cleaners, medicines and matches **LOCKED UP** and out of your reach."

"I will have to start using the **Keep Out Cupboard** that's above our fridge for all of our poisonous cleaners and matches. I'm also going to have to make sure that all of our medicines have **SAFETY LIDS** on them."

"You must promise me that you will **NEVER** play with matches, and that you will stay away from poisonous cleaners and medicines."

"How can I tell what's poisonous and what isn't?" I asked.

"You can always ask me," said my mom, "but if I'm not around, and you see something that you aren't sure of, tell your hands **NOT** to touch it!"

"When you put your bike helmet on and go out to ride your bike without bubble wrap, you must be **EXTRA** careful to always:

• Watch for cars.

• Make eye contact with the drivers of the cars so that you know they see you.

• Ride safely and pay attention **ALL** of the time."

"Without bubble wrap,
you'll have to wear your bike
helmet when you Pogo."

"My bike helmet can be a Pogo
helmet too?" I asked.

"Absolutely," said my mom.

"Finally," she said, "without bubble wrap, you must be much more careful when you are going up and down our stairs. Make sure you **slow down** a bit, and always use the hand rail."

"Why didn't we just do the **BASICS** in the first place?" I asked.
"Then you wouldn't have needed to buy all of that bubble wrap."

"Because **I** am The Bubble Wrap Queen!" said my mom.
"But since there is no more bubble wrap to buy and you know all about the
BASICS, my reign as queen has come to an end."

She handed me a small piece of bubble wrap.

"What's this for?" I asked.

"To POP!" she said.

A Special Note to Parents

As a pediatrician, parenting expert *and* as the proud mother of three, I find that parents today (myself included) dedicate a good portion of each day trying to insure the safety of our children. And for good reason – because whether it's in the kitchen, the car, or anywhere else our kids routinely go, keeping kids safe is a parent's number one priority. While in no way lessening the importance of having serious safety discussions with children, I am also, however, a firm believer that teaching kids important life (and in this case, safety) lessons does not have to be a boring affair. All too often, those of us who take our adult responsibilities the most seriously make the unfortunate mistake of taking the fun out of them as well – leaving our children bored, disinterested, and far less likely to actually remember what it is we want them to know about being aware of their surroundings and knowing how to be safe in common situation.

In *The Bubble Wrap Queen*, Julia Cook has created a book that is bursting with some very important basic childhood safety rules that are well worth focusing on, learning, teaching and promoting. They include:

- **Automobile Awareness Safety:** Never allow your child to play in or around cars. In only a relatively few minutes, the inside of a parked car can become swelteringly (and life-threateningly) hot. Additionally, cars can tragically be bumped into gear, children can be trapped in trunks, and it is unfortunately all too easy for a child playing behind a car to be overlooked.

- **Automobile Crash Safety:** Motor vehicle crashes remain the number one killer of kids ages 1-14. Fortunately, children can be safely and easily protected from this risk by simply insuring that they are properly restrained in a well-installed and age/size appropriate car

continued on next page

seat each and every time they get in a car. With added safety features such as higher rear-facing weight limits, side impact crash protection, and the ability to use the internal 5-point restraint to as high as 80 pounds in some newer seats – parents can keep their kids safer than ever…and without resorting to bubble wrap.

• **Poison Prevention:** In addition to buying and storing medicines in child-proof containers out of the reach of kids, it is important to be on the lookout for other potential poisons around the home as well. According to Safe Kids Worldwide, over half of the poisonings of children under the age of five are from such non-pharmaceutical products such as plants, cleaning products, pesticides, alcohol and even art supplies and toys. Despite taking all the best precautions, it's nevertheless well worth your while to have the national poison control hotline phone number readily available.
It is 800-222-1222.

• **Bicycle Safety:** Make it a rule in your household that anything your child rides on with wheels – from a tricycle to a dirt bike - requires a well-fitting bicycle helmet, and pay close attention to insure that your child learns and respects the rules of the road before venturing down the sidewalk or across his/her first driveway.

While *The Bubble Wrap Queen* undoubtedly makes learning these and other such safety messages more fun, the underlying messages are no laughing matter because the more your child enjoys reading and learning about them, the more they stick. And the more they stick, the more likely they are to save lives!

– Dr. Laura A. Jana
Pediatrician, Nationally Recognized Parenting Expert , Award Winning Author , and Founder of Practical Parenting Consulting and The Doctor Spock Company